THE LAST FALCON
AND SMALL ORDINANCE

First published in 2010 by
The Dedalus Press
13 Moyclare Road
Baldoyle
Dublin 13
Ireland

www.dedaluspress.com

Editor: Pat Boran

ISBN 978 1 906614 28 7

Dedalus Press titles are represented in North America
by Syracuse University Press, Inc., 621 Skytop Road,
Suite 110, Syracuse, New York 13244, and in the UK by
Central Books, 99 Wallis Road, London E9 5LN

Cover image © Blair Howard / iStockphoto.com

The Dedalus Press receives financial assistance from
The Arts Council / An Chomhairle Ealaíon

the arts
council
chomhairle
ealaíon

funding
literature
artscouncil.ie

The Last Falcon
and Small Ordinance

Paul Perry

DEDALUS PRESS
DUBLIN, IRELAND

ACKNOWLEDGEMENTS

Grateful acknowledgement is made to the editors of the following publications where some of these poems first appeared:

The Irish Times, The Stinging Fly, The Oxfam 2008 Calendar, Salmon: A Journey 1982-2007, Janera: The Voice of Global Nomads, The Irish American Post, Southword, Revival, Poetry Ireland Review, 3 A.M. and *dogmatika.*

The author wishes to acknowledge with gratitude the assistance of The Arts Council of Northern Ireland for a Bursary in Literature, 2007 and The Arts Council of Ireland for a Multi-Annual Bursary in Literature, 2007—2009.

for Aoife & Bláithín & Fionn
& for my brother David
who asked me to write about it

Contents

'The poet is a brother speaking to a brother of a moment of their other lives, a moment that had been buried beneath the dust of the busy world.'
—Edith Sitwell

'And I must borrow every changing shape
To find expression ….'
—T.S. Eliot, 'Portrait of a Lady'

Promise

You get off the train
in another nowhere town
and are welcomed home.

The wind leads you
to a road and you start
to walk.

Where you came from
is nowhere like this.

A man is pushing
a bike. He tells you
the rain is on its way,
but you don't see.

He offers you
a place to sleep.

You keep going
to where there are fields.

Not far from a river,
someone is calling out.

A woman is standing in
the doorway of a house.
She sees through you.

In her silence,
there is something
of a promise,

something
which suggests
you could
if you wanted
become again
the person
you wished to be.

You can hear the voices
of children,
their laughter.
You can choose to walk on.

You've been travelling
a long time.

Before you speak
the first words of the day
you can rest.

The world is waking.
And the morning is welling onto your lips.

Speak.
Say something.
You can still be healed.

To the Future

in the morning you are woken
by the engine of loneliness
you have lived such a short time
you have lived such a long time

each day stretches out
like the barrel of a gun
lovers die everyday
and the ennui of sirens and alarms

makes you nostalgic
for Vera Lynn's 'Harbour Lights'
or the black and white's
on Sunday afternoons

highways and hotels
and the new neon crucifix
keep the city what it is
and still where else would you be

not Tangiers
death has a new army
but we still need to love one another
or get through today anyway

the future is already here
and even if the cars are crashing
and the money's tight
someone says I love you

and someone else means it
there'll be new gods
to curse and disbelieve
new sports and books to read

if you listen carefully
the letters and stories
are already gathering
like a group intent

on demonstrating
something like solidarity
illicitly or not
they may be our only hope

Dawn Sun

if people had smuggled animals
onto the bus I hadn't noticed
the fields were silver in the dawn
church-goers wrapped themselves in their myths
and out of the earth the old cries came
no one noticed heeded or believed
nor in the road's plaintive appeal

so be it … the dead lined the way
waving farewell or …
hats were doffed smiles no not smiles …
workers stood up from the fields
and watched our passing
some with envy some with regret
the smell of schnapps was something we shared
there were no songs but heavy sleep
pale eyes expelled smoke

and the dawn sun startled us with its cold fire
my words had already banished me
but I hoped our bodies might meet
before the scrap-yard of longing
closed its bloody gates

I was unsure in the new city
tripping over memory's shoelaces
when the light of mid-morning
warmed my feet
and I danced over the river

you were surprised by my voice
calling out to you
on the street
but you should not have been
that is what it had been doing
for a long time
since the time we first met
and before

The Last Falcon and Small Ordinance

No one was there when I returned, not a soul
though each one of the settlers' personal effects remained:
some wrapped in dust, some overgrown with grass.
Axe, file, compass. Scuppet, dice and pipe.

Iron pots rusted. Maps and books spoiled by rain.
Words sank into the soil never to be heard again:
words like *love* and *peace*. In this moon-shaken dawn
there was no evidence of a struggle, no sign of violence.

On a tree in Roman letters *CRO* was carved and so I ventured
toward the point of the creek, but again found no sign
of the settlers, nor of the last falcon and small ordinance
I had left them with. The colony was lost; it had disappeared.

The maps of the New World were to be my task, but
there would linger about this place a shadow,
one which no cartographer could draw and the name
Roanoke became the ghost of a name. What then

must have happened remains but a mystery.
Was it a massacre or an assimilation of sorts?
In these my last years, I have often wondered
while making maps of land for Raleigh's tenants in Kylmore.

I have wondered and dreamt, dreamt and wondered.
But nothing, no answer nor salve has come to me,
no visitation of grace either, whether I have prayed or not.
I have lived since then a quiet life. I know my granddaughter

to be the first English child born to the land, a fact
which should make me proud; but it does not.
Instead I'm left with a feeling not unlike guilt,
albeit a guilt tinged with something like awe and regret,

a feeling of being alone under the old world's white skies.
And even if my memory fails me, even if the voices
fade, I can still see ingots at the bottom of the sea
and hedgerows on fire. I see too how history cannot map

whatever losses the heart has held and I hear cries
for help in the forest or rather an echo thereof,
and within the undulations of this wild landscape
I fear it simply to be the wind exclaiming

or my own faltering mind telling me something
it ought not to have forgotten, a clue perhaps to what
may have happened, but the words, whatever words there were,
are still too feint to make out, still too distant to hear.

A River in the Irish Midlands

the stones shine like silver
and sink into your hands
slip into knots and become
the anchor of a longing
that will not break its bounds

where water is alive with voices
and sunlight wickers and shakes
the fronds and gold flowers
rain's witness calls out a clue
to the secret of the river

and a girl's drowned eyes
extinguished sometime blue
ripple and rise into the net
of an anyday Sunday memory
what they say is simple:

no one fishes here anymore

Reservations

What you told me
on that drive
through the Everglades
made me feel
as much a prisoner

as you did when
your mother
placed you,
a gentle phrase,
for something

more barbaric,
in that home,
did you say home,
or institution
for troubled teenagers,

wearing an orange suit
like a criminal;
this coming from a woman
who called us
to berate me

for hiding a series
of rare first editions
in the walls of our house
on McCulloch
and thereby spending

all our money.
I felt as if I were
living someone else's life
or that I was
a fiction

in someone else's
imagination.
Later we'd go
to the reservation
to gamble

or drive through Royal Palm,
Flamingo, Shark Valley
and Everglade City:
a subtropical preserve
of saw grass prairies

and cypress swamp;
that too seemed unreal
made real only
by their description,
by their (re) telling:

pineland hardwood
hammocks.
Even now I sometimes
wake and hear the call
of an egret

though I know
that there can be
no such thing
outside this window:
no egret, no wood-stork,

no roseate spoonbill.
What I do know
is that someone else
shares my bed now.
She has her own past,

has inhabited her own
fragile eco-systems;
while she sleeps
there is out there a wilderness
of half-remembered lives.

Some of it is
endangered.
Some of it dying.
Sometimes,
you can hear it

cry out
in the form
of the great blue heron.
Look:
it's landing

on a body
of water, and
you, idle,
resigned, but appreciative
are standing by its banks.

Zero Point

I closed my eyes
And told you what I saw
You said no
But I kept on

The garden showered in light
The eucalyptus towering and diving
And waking us with its myths
Its stories of my grandfather in Spain

At war his poetry and how he took
When he returned to Ireland
His life and the life of the one he loved
And in broad daylight

Imagine the family's shame
Which is why I am writing in the dark
And why you are wondering
About the zero-point of our love

I don't blame you
Well maybe a little
Another reason I keep talking
As though I had a theory of everything

And why you think to live for ever
No great shakes
Too many full moons you say
Is that I've often wondered

About what will be in the long to come
That is when at night my lungs
Aren't filling with water
Nearly wrote eyes instead of lungs

And before I forget
Today I saw a hungry blackbird
It's cold you know
Colder than a coal miner's face

Rubbed its orange beak
Into my hand
Felt like the time
You put your hand

On the tensile fence
On the farm of your childhood
Or your grandmother's
My merula to your moses

Amen
How this turned into a memory
Of you I can't say
And all of a sudden

My date palm
My caucasian chalk circle
I your gentile
Your barbarian

I imagine we meet
In one or another future
Where it happens again
On an old road

I throw stones
At your glasshouse
Take the shards from your hands
And let the bird fly

Visiting Hours

I am driving northwards across the border
into south Down and farther north, driving
through a lean vegetation into summer,
golden and sweet, allowing my mind to wander

to familiar and unfamiliar places. A map
lies on the passenger seat beside me.
I've reached for it, but am distracted
by the ten white crosses on the embankment

before Newry which makes me think
of you and your troubled time: how
you'd hid beneath the bedclothes,
a starched white sheet and old blue blanket,

one which reminds me of our childhood.
'How do I know it's you?' you'd said
from under the dishevelled canopy you had created.
'How do I know you are not just a voice in my head?'

I've tapped you on the back to stir you
from your week-long disturbances, shifting
from sleep to waking dream. You groan
and move and peek out at me from under the covers.

Chocolate bar wrappers and sweet packets
litter the bed-side table. Bottles of water and
juice stand half finished. You sit up, finally,
not with the mock machine gun you fired

the first time I went to visit you.
'It could happen,' you bellowed dispensing
several rounds at the other patients.
This time your one caveat is:

It's worse than one flew over the cuckoo's nest.
Said without the grin, but with the doleful
look you carry on occasion, the same no doubt
when you met in Spain two men from the IRA,

two men you say, who followed you there
after three years surveillance to interrogate
and torture you. I had just started to work
on the border when you fell into your troubled

state, filling out funding applications for peace
and reconciliation. 'Peace money,' is what
they called it, as if such an ambition had a price tag.
I wondered now as I drove across borders

what solicitude it would take to bring you back
to who you were. Not, I imagined, a doctor
who asked me if I thought what you talked
about had happened, had really happened. This

is your story, but I know you're not going to tell
it, not again, not with the relish and obsession
you did while still in it. Your time
inside was frightening, but amusing too.

When you were called for dinner once
and I went to leave, you pointed to a bed
and told me I was welcome. The next day
you recounted how the paramilitaries

had administered pain killers. Truth drugs,
you called them. You talked about how
they kept you against your will, how they
tried to drown you. I turn the radio on,

but it serves no distraction and so I drive,
drive on with the thought that this then is the legacy
of the conflict, or one of its legacies.
That after the bombings, the shootings, the warfare

and ceasefires, after peace and reconciliation,
what we, what some of us, are left with
is a man in a hospital bed, afraid for his life.
Drive on. And I do, into unknown territory,

marked with flags, unlike the mind
which is an unmarked maze, past Ballymena,
towards Coleraine, past the bunting
and the painted curb-stones towards

the end of another journey,
the end of another reverie and what I am
left with is the same uneasy satisfaction
I feel when leaving you on those occasions

after visiting hours are over, namely
the questions: what is real, what happened,
what really happened? And dear brother,
part of living, part of the struggle, our struggle,

I suppose, is that no matter how much we think
about it, interrogate our pasts or actions,
no matter how much we beseech you
or each other, we'll never really know.

You are the boy on the rocks

after Henri Rousseau

You are the boy on the rocks
You are the boy riding bare back
No saddle or stirrup or horse

You are the boy on the rocks
Picked up by the wind
And flung heavenward

You are the boy on the rocks
Tip-toeing through dreams
With gypsies and tigers

You are the boy on the rocks
Not happy or sad
Stepping through worlds

You are the boy on the rocks
Lost and longed for
Without a past or future

You are the boy on the rocks

To the Book of Kells

He woke after what seemed
like a hundred years of sleep,
found his clothes, recently
returned to him, walked down

the stairs and out into the daylight.
He walked slowly. It felt
like he was walking on the moon.
He rose and wavered,

floated, sprang from one foot
to the other. Everything
sped by him. Cars, people,
and dreams. His own thoughts

remained deliberate, careful.
Past the brewery, down by the river
shining in sunlight, he walked.
When he reached the Book in its tower

he gazed at its arcane colours
and curlicues and heard the vellum
like wind through a field soughing
and shifting. He thought of the island

Iona and the visions of the monks and
then of his own recent and strange
imaginings. Fantastical paranoia.
IRA plots, accusations, kidnappings

and tortures. After swimming
in the sea of the Book, he shook
himself dry and walked slowly
along the river, dark now, but still

with hints of gold and green.
No one noticed when he returned
or that he had been gone
in the first place. He went to the bathroom,

removed his clothes, took his robe
and went back to bed. It was not
night, but he closed his eyes anyway
and entered not darkness but

another world where the Book began
to grow, gain strength, and as he fell
into a fitful sleep, to thread and stitch
its way tightly and colourfully into his dreams.

Desire

night waits

for any small proclamation
a confession

it is patient
stone-like in its fortitude

it wants all longing
it has waited before

desire will be its captive

Between One Death and Another

in the house you lived
between one death and another

a cliff   the sea
a narrow path

forget the mirrors
they have all been taken away

no birds sing here
a bedroom without warmth

no one grows old here either
the dead are welcomed

they have lost and lost
one heirloom: an old man's watch

keeps ticking
cover it if you must

swallow the time
if you can

Only at Night

the calendar flies from its stoop
like a frightened crow

and the days fall from each other
only at night do the hours grow

seem longer
allow you the chance to breath

dusk lends you time
and history's ashes are whistling

in the air
in the wind

in the ...
you name it

no more honey
in the hives then

you'll not outstare the lightning
only at night

can you think and when you do
the mirrors shut their doors

and your life a maze
presents itself with only one way out

what you're left with is
desire

sometimes there's nothing (left)
to praise
but the darkness

Black Dust

no, it's November again
the golden falling month

and that black dust
those leaves
are words you did not use
or misused
or forgot

we'll all be gone soon
the spirits surround us
call them memories if you like
if you can't say the word:
ghost   soul   spirit

the past emerges like a river
dressed as a circus come to town

there are the posters
and the smell of unhappy animals
always
angels left behind
or a woman with wings anyway

it's not the parrot I know
or the owl or doves
trailing out of the tent like smoke rising

it will be forgotten
they have closed their gates
your enemies

the dead
are always restless

give them the site
the circus
the sky's height
and crows
surrounding Timon's tree
all the salt hours

listen
I'm ready now

Oklahoma

What must you have thought
when they summoned you
to the sergeant's office?
When they told you not

unsympathetically
that not only had your mother died
but that she was the one
who had taken her own life.

What must you have thought
when they told you that she
had left no note or explanation,
but that you were of course,

entitled to a leave of absence,
the irony! No, you argue, no,
that could not be she, your mother,
our mother, she was not the kind to ...

The officers offered their condolences
and said you could go back
to Oklahoma that very day.
Why, you asked, would you want

to go to Oklahoma, a place
you'd never been. To make the arrangements.
To bury your mother.
'My mother's not in Oklahoma.

My mother's never
been to Oklahoma nor has my mother
ever had the inclination
to go to Oklahoma,' you might have said.

What must you have thought
when they stuttered strange replies
and shuffled papers on the desk and
asked you again your name?

Already three years in the Marines,
what must you have thought brother?
A feeling of loss without loss.
An endless expanse of water

and a horizon with nothing on it
but its own perpetual extension?
Like love, maybe, or one version of it.
Something which reminds me of the time

a lover told me once I was not
the person she thought I was.
What must you have thought?
Perhaps of the other private,

the one with your name, you his,
how he would now be summoned
to be told what you had been told
to deny like you had denied,

to shake his head at a world
full of mistaken identities,
summonings, revelations,
recantations and invitations

to Oklahoma, Oklahoma,
for a leave of absence,
a leave of absence,
taken, not taken.

Asphalt

I was living in Providence when it happened.
It was an ordinary day in Autumn. I'd heard
on the radio that the U2 concert tickets
were going on sale. My neighbour Wade

drove downtown to the Civic Centre
and together we stood in line.
How what happened happened, I don't know.
There was no pre-meditation.

We waited in line. We got our tickets.
We celebrated. For some reason, the scalpers
bothered us. They wanted to know if
we were buying or selling. Now everything

happens quickly. We go back home.
We must have talked, but I don't remember.
What I do remember is getting two other tickets.
Dire Straits, can you believe. And putting

them into the envelopes in which the U2
tickets were sold. Then we drove back down
to the Civic Centre. I remember walking up
the steps of the Civic Centre and feeling ill.

Strange, but when I look back at it now
it is as if I had no choice in the matter:
that's how those younger years look to me now—
a series of events that happened to me.

Pretty soon, I'm running from some small-timers
with a wad of cash clenched in my fist.
We'd swopped the tickets and resold them,
lord knows why, nothing planned, nothing thought through.

A man chased me.
I jumped into the car and told Wade to move it.
A man, the man who chased us, not the man
I had sold the tickets to, not the small,

fat man in a track-suit, another man,
a bigger man, a younger, faster, stronger
man then leapt onto the car, onto the roof-rack
and smashed the back windscreen in with his foot.

Shit, I was scared.
Mumbling to myself and shouting at Wade
to drive faster, faster, until the car swung
this way and that and then the man hanging

onto the roof-rack fell onto the hot asphalt
and slowly struggled to his feet.
We kept driving.
We drove from one town to the next.

With the money, burning in my hand,
we had the windscreen fixed. We ate pizza
and thought we saw the touts and ran.
We ran down one street and down another.

We hid behind a building.
I said, 'I don't want to die like this.'
And thought the beating we might get
could be a shooting. We trembled

and shook and walked finally after an age
from where we were hiding into the warm
New England air, relieved and sweating and repentant.
I shaved my beard. Wade got a hair cut.

We hid the car with a friend and returned
to Providence by train. I still can't figure out
why we did what we did. There was a party
that night. Our story spread. Wade dropped acid

and took a bad trip, seeing the fallen man
wherever he looked. I took, in the following weeks,
phone-calls from friends, mostly crank-calls,
people pretending to be gangsters.

I can remember my fear as something acrid,
but I still can't figure out why we did what we did.
I can't even believe that it was me. I can remember
it though exactly and acutely ...

Like pain: the car, stuttering into gear, the tickets
slipped into their envelope, the steps of the Civic Centre
crumbling beneath me ...
& Wade's curls falling onto the barber shop floor,

all of it wavering in a slow dizzy dance
much like the man who fell towards the asphalt
which burned beneath him and was ready, ready
to carry him, carry us all to somewhere we'd never been.

Tattoos and Books

Once I worked the night shift at a library.
I liked the quiet, the books, the occasional visit
from a friend. There was me, Karl and a security guard,
a man who liked to patrol the stacks

and return with the pornography
some students left behind. He carried a radio
and received news about violent incidents
in the area which he liked to share with us.

He was a pretty un-likeable guy, the way
he took such pleasure in the casual bloodiness
of his reports, what with his wide grin and swagger.
Karl was different, a small German man

with a voice full of the echoes
of emptying streets and a tattoo on his arm
which meant only one thing.
Together the three of us watched

the garden of the clock grow wild
and waited each in our own different ways,
a student, a security guard, a librarian.
Karl and the guard took off early each night

leaving me, I didn't mind, to pull down
the shutters and put on the alarm.
I knew some students hid in the stacks
to study late, force themselves into an all-nighter.

I had none of their diligence or drive.
I walked instead to a bar
where a girl I knew worked,
my head full of the guard's stories

and Karl's silences and the words
from the books I'd read, words
which never saved a soul, but surface
even now like the sounds you make

during one of your rants and ravings,
just another story really, not saving us,
but getting us through whatever late night
we have to endure. You said I should

write your story, put words to it,
in a book, I don't think you had a poem
in mind, if that is what this is,
a book which could be turned into a film,

which would make you some money
so you could buy a house,
you even said I could live there too,
charitable soul, a book which could sit

on the shelves of a library much like the one
I worked in, in Providence, all those years ago
where the security guard grinned at his radio,
leafed through his pornography, where

I waited for the clock to cover its face
and let me loose, into leafy portentous Providence,
where Karl kept his sleeves rolled down,
even on a warm night like this.

On the Way to Three-Rock

What it was that lead me
through the fields and into forest
I can't say, but whatever it was
it felt like a compulsion;

in other words, I had no choice
in the matter. This may have
happened before, but somewhere else.
In the forest there was the dense

smell of pine, underfoot the crunch
of kindle and out of it like smoke
rising from a dead fire
came the fluttering of birds and

their voices above me in the trees.
Suddenly I was there in the clearing,
high up, watching a boy pitch a tent
and a girl watch him. They fumbled

together in the dark, they held
each other like first-time lovers.
They did not see me; I was not
to be seen. Besides what would

I have said to myself: that the mist
in the morning will be cold and
the moon, it will stay
hanging in the sky at least until dawn?

Counterpoint: Vasks' Distant Light

the music reminds me
of a night
when the car
was repossessed

it's a sad
and frantic melody
full of sleeplessness and
misgiving

the knot
we tied
was as much within me
as it was on paper

what I will admit to
and not grudgingly
is a certain amount of admiration
for the way

you got into our newly
bought used second car
a lesson for the folly
of those who aspire

to the middle classes
and the way you chased
the repossessed car
which held among other personal effects

some new poems
you had made
I commend
your driving

and your reckless panic
to reclaim the fruits
of your imagination
from the carcass

of the car
we had bought together
we swerved this way
and that

and then when the re-possessor
stopped the car
at a gas station
and got out of it to pay for gas

you jumped out
and took what was yours
not the car
you had long fallen into arrears

but the poems you had written
precious cargo, no?
we read them later
over wine and laughed

at your ingenuity
and driving skills
that was before
all the trouble we had

but let's not go there now
my point here
is the music
how mysteriously

it calls up what went before
and helps us
to put images to the sound
stories to the melody

however painful
however unsure
how it counterpoints
our present lives

with the past
which has after all
made us
who we are

Winter

Winter arrives secretly,
puts a chill into your dreams
you hardly notice, makes
you shake and think

of somewhere else.
The leaves fall
from the trees,
they say something to you like

leave, get out while you can.
Before children arrive,
before chaos comes
before the forgetting of what you

wanted to do with yourself,
once upon a time, dawns.
A friend calls,
says lets hit the town,

get outta here, go drink,
meet women,
leave it all behind.
It's not even someone you know.

You go gambling.
You lose. You forget where
you parked the car.
You hitch

and wake up somewhere
where it's summer.
It's what you wanted.
The girl beside you

speaks another language and
slowly you begin to understand.
It's about unpaid bills
and outstanding debts.

It's nothing to do
with living for the now,
whatever that is.
You roll over onto your side

but before you do
you catch a glimpse
of her dissatisfaction:
it's in her eyes,

they have something
of winter about them.
They put a chill
into your dreams.

They make you think
of somewhere else.
Instead of running
you tell her yes

you will put the trash out,
but not now, please not now.

solstice

he was scared
and ashamed
he thought
whatever he got
he deserved

she asked him to lie
by her
in the hospital bed
to be with her
and ...

all because
she didn't get his message
hard to believe
even now
that is how it started

truth is
they were always fighting
but still loved
each other
and how ...

the guard he could tell
wanted to beat
the shit out of him
he eyed him
and the doctor

she couldn't look
at him
but said she was so
sorry
this had happened to her

they agreed to tell
people she was
in a car crash
he wanted to die
and lay

in prison
on the ground
shaking in an open cell
one black man
held the phone

down his pants
and said now
who needs to make a call
when he got home
he tried his best

that xmas
was good
they took care of each other
but someone knew their secret
and there can be no secrets

he wonders
if they knew now
what they knew
then
what might have happened …

as if it mattered
and so after a drive
from one city to another
after the winter solstice
the world again came apart

she left ...
he stood trying
his body's weight on a rope
in the room
she brought her poems to

he still remembers the shame
the love cowardice
and pain
back then it was what
made them who they were

Tender Accomplice

I walk towards the sound
it is at first indecipherable
inscrutable
gradually it becomes clearer
the sound of voices
the sound of people I know
and do not know

perceptibly the sound rises
like the wind on the lake
it picks up and darkens my vision
it dizzies the forest
and covers the pathway
it turns the world into a storm
and I turn and turn again

I turn to walk
from the sound
I turn to silence
tender accomplice
which is nowhere
and falls slowly and darkly
like a late snow

Of Work and Longing

The roses are bleeding

Let them bleed

This summer everything is wrong
This summer ...

You can't escape yourself

Your co-worker is asleep
Amongst the bales of peat

Bless her teenage heart

And you don't have the answers
When it comes to clematis or bougainvillea

Every plant you've owned has died
Bar the cactus
They've tried
But have only survived on sweat and tears

This summer is spent

You blow your pay-check

There are so many auto-biographies
Too many

What's your story
What's the one thing you would tell the people

Jury, God, Buddha, brother, loved one, death-bed attendee

What a beautiful language the horticulturists had
Love lies bleeding and such

You can't pretend to be of their ilk

You know roads and asphalt
You know lone nights
And long walks home

You know the pawn store and they know you

Who'll take you in
Who'll read to you
Now you need to sleep

You know neon and its barbs
(you know the museum of infinite strangeness)

Once you might have been …

The roses are bleeding
Let them bleed

For a time …
It's the only true thing

Orphan Way

the street is no longer
its chipped paving gone
its long eyelashes clipped
street you are invisible

we did not worship enough
at your beckoning
we took you for granted
on your stones we walked

but without reverence or guile
old vanished place
where did you go
did we offend

it was a road for sinning
but we're all grown up now
no need for your harlot cries
your corner boys

you're somewhere else now
orphan way
and the only ghosts
who walk your way

are happy ghosts
what choice do they have
you hold their past
precious in your grip

A Thousand Years of Myth

the summer was a short one
even in Wiesbaden
thunderstorms came
into the jealous gutters
paint and plaster fell with zeal

in your grandfather's house
there were war medals
a black cross preserved in a glass case
and silence among the pines

an aunt's house
displayed a rare caged bird
books of unread literature

all sorts of historical horrors preceded us
all manner of personal ones lay ahead

the ruin of our hearts
memory's wreckage
the past's traffic to here

every betrayal is recalled
nothing is forgiven
nothing forgotten

the old gods waken
we need them

the muse asks for more

summer is short
a thousand years of myth
guide us

they stand open-mouthed
applauding our resolve

to make the same ancient mistakes
once again
recalling every betrayal
reminding us
nothing is forgiven
nothing forgotten

Kite String

when he put
the gun
to my head

I thought
of a childhood
summer

in Wicklow
I felt the
wind

tug
at the kite
string

in my hand
I saw
the blood

stained
wool
on the barb

and the
chicken eggs
warm

and
soft
in my hands

I felt them
too
once more

How Many Years in Germany?

sunlight on an oil-slicked road
two boys on a motorbike
hills and an abandoned train-station
fields music singing

what else
so much else
each road will lead here
everything is connected

but what if we stop the boys now
stop the motorbike
what if the oil-slicked road
becomes ... a rainbow

in some far-off field
of sunflowers
it's possible
then maybe what's about to happen

does not happen
or happens else-time
when the rainbow has faded
the sunflowers fallen

and the singing music fields
are somewhere else
somewhere far away from here
then what

then what of your everything is connected
of your each road ...oil-slicked
rain-bowed sun-flowered
what then

Prophecy

after Sandor Csoori

the last winter will arrive
with the sound of bells

and wheels covering cobblestones
horses too will neigh and whinny

from their tar-black nostrils
eternity will pour its lullaby

men and women will declaim
of their innocence

and sink into the shadows
children will take to the streets

fire will arrive
light the lakes and water

no god will condemn
no god will forgive

but people will burn
all day and all night

and there will be
no resurrection

Whatever

Back then you were full of impetuous
passion, all or nothing promises,
like the hot Mediterranean sun in July.
Said things like now or never.

Words were like drums.
And you climbed all the trees.
Painted your face
and tried to fly a thousand times.

Clover and honeysuckle
you tangled in and drank.
Chickadees chirped for you
and the nights conspired.

Somewhere in the haze,
the drop-zone addiction
of the now said 'stop' and the fields
once green grew overgrown.

The self remaindered itself,
met its image in a cul-de sac
of confession and retreated
to a place without adjectives.

Not that it started you praying,
but it did make you a little blind.
Your handwriting grew large enough
to make out but not understand.

Now you make love to any man
with an echo of the 'only you'.

You forget their names as quickly
as the light goes out

and walk alone by the canal
to where you once lived.
That's what happens.
A life of wrong turns and detours

takes you away from where
you thought you were going.
Blame chance if you like.
Blame youth or the midday sun.

Blame Tantalus and the golden dog.
Whatever. The main thing is to remember
what you once had and pine,
go on, keep crying,

now you're the girl at the circus
the one without her candy-floss.
Your grey eyes returned me
to where I am. Still bitter,

still mad, but not so dangerous to know,
no? The images you sell, if only
you worshipped them, bang on the doors
of your dreams. There's one

of a violin, or a man playing a violin,
two birds rest on his lap, the music
takes him above the city,
and away from the names

you once gave to their love.

Somewhere there's a river

what am I do with this ...
the impossibility of spring

what am I ...
the cherry blossoms

fall and
                    fly
across the ground

they come towards me like
something from the past

all that longing
long forgot

I thought the muse
had left me

left me to be a happier man

what is it you want from me anyway

my silence

but not before you seduced the moon

that night by the river
because somewhere
there is a river

and what of the cake

what are we like

some kind of Hansel and Gretel
not children
but be-forested and
hand in hand

we knew where we were going

we knew

nothing

what is it you want from me anyway

look somewhere there is a river

listen to the swans on its surface

they glide towards your majestic hands

what is it you want from me

nothing

what is I want from you

everything

                    and then some

well then should we not have gone to the river
where the swans were waiting

where we fed them cake

I can't find anything

I should be beyond all of this
but no
it shakes me
it takes me
away
from where I should be

as if I ever belonged here

somewhere there's a river
meet me there

what can you remember of the night
do we forget
is it easier to forget

it's darkening
dark now

and the photographs
are they gone

what evidence do we need
to forgo the desire

somewhere there's a river
even the swans

if I close my eyes

what I remember is your voice in the darkness
its gentle strangeness
to me
its tender appeal

what I remember is
meet me by the river

are you letting me go
have you let me go then

if I close my eyes

will the formality of the night be all
high priestess

will …

it is wrong
I am wrong

what I remember is your voice

if I …

here the cherry blossoms
are falling like rain
like snow
now

like every drop of desire
left in me

they don't stop falling
they fall
and fall

I wish they'd bury me

in your hands
if I …

cherry blossoms

and somewhere there's a river

and snow
your voice in the darkness

your hands
your beautiful hands
and
swans

swans
touch me too

By Antakalnis Cemetery

what will I tell my heart
that it doesn't already know

our earthly duties
keep my feet on the ground

but you still believe in eternity
now you have me thinking

about the chaos inside
and trying the word soul

again on my lips
for the taste

but you have better reasons
and deeper motivations

the pale hands of your mother
for example and when

we walked past the graveyard
where Jurga is buried

you picked up a mayfly
and told us how they could take flight

we knew then someone has a sense
of humour because after you

nature lover tossed it into the air
it landed on the road with a thump

but enough of that I want you to tell
me about the mirror in front of you

or the door we need to walk through
to realise a new imaginative landscape

we need to know ourselves
we need silence too

but it scares me to think
what I might find

what can come of it
the heart is in chaos

it is morning already
we could have kept talking

and never mentioned
the word love

we could have
we could have

Bull's tongue slumgullion

I.

bull's tongue slumgullion
gull fly onion bullion
slum tongue yum sum
tongue salad hum ya
curd roe red ho
strip tease please no
taxi man say so
no no knife life
tid bit what bit in it
bread ha well fed grave
stones grey stones no
bones burn tones
pig ears who hears
fear tears comrade dog
stop barking comrade
dog stop barking
harking and parking
your tongue's bull
slumgullion hungry
pumpkin drum coming
candle spigots
soviet spiddles
has dog comrade gone
doc what
sick you when when
slumgullion gulley cat
beggar beggar bye bye
what human nests
walk through
who who achoo

why what tank you
gesundheit it's my kite
slumgullion fly night
farewell out of sight
out of sight in mind
what mind my mind
mind gullion birch tree
tree climb
heim climb weh tune
home now hymn song
say so where to
here so

because

II.

and then I dreamt
no it was a nightmare

my fingers came unstuck
I gathered their bloody stumps

and announced the emergency to my wife
who shrugged

and continued to cut the wig
on our daughter's head

you are the only one
I know who will
have something to say
about these matters

write to me

Morning Song

decide one way or the other
　　　it's difficult you suppose

light hurts the eyes
　　　that have not slept

but stay in darkness
　　　and please no more sack cloth

the church is on its knees again
　　　no place for cupid

the only shrine is the one
　　　in my brother's room for Our Lady

images proliferate
　　　grow like mushrooms

the wax is heavy with pennies
　　　forget heaven

I'm talking about the poormouth
　　　who was your grandmother

and her dark faith
　　　the only music she heard

was the night drawing
　　　the curtain on itself

the doors are locked
　　　and morning is waiting

cupped in your hands
      like a blade of grass

your lips are blowing on to

only say the word

what we don't say to each other

        is lost

        somewhere

  in the soil

        where tomorrow's   dog digs

here's the bone

        good boy

        juicy and bloody   and fresh

everything said

        is screened

the words light up

           when you walk through security
the way
     you walk
          through
me

        and I become a host again

for all

                the rabbling   regret

        of forgotten   gods

        above us   the sun
is
        ready
                        to
            fall

        reach out

                no

        your eyes   widen

at the possibility

        of owning time again

        but do you have the password

it's like a sinking coin

        a promise

                    laid   bare

a memory

        dissolving

in a glass of water

is your thirst slaked

    your philosophy true

    communicate

to me

    without words then

remake the sound

      with your eyes

      with your lips

          remake me

Aubade

what love there is
is out of reach
sour rain and mint
leaves its history
in the air
but not for long
everything is disappearing
even the smell of you
marzipan desire sex
the distance between each word
wants nothing more
than its own
right to silence
I believe in
the folk-tale of pain
I believe
we will never
say these words
to another again
salted lips
I'll have to relearn
an older language
don't bother thinking
of Carthage
Galway
how about Dublin
York Street
Number 9.3
sign here
general labourer
we will never say
these words again

tenements and memory
hiding in archives of rain
what apparitions
the moon dispels
are dream induced
and full of tears
we'll never talk
about the past
like we once did
the dry paper of our letters
is the kindle and lie
of early hearts
whatever the fortune tellers say
whatever your horoscope
predicts there'll be no record
save for the oblique
images of regret
and long-distance phone-calls
crows kept me company
on those dawn walks home
all time wants is a chance
to redeem itself
and pick the right colour
for its shroud
not a coloured coat
something white
and historical
children and intimates
are chasing the gods
we let go
eyes blur the words
meet me in the place
they have left
it's a gallery of flesh
a body without
the breath to say no

Love Poem

not eyes
don't start with the eyes
otherwise they will haunt you
besides you might say smoke
or water or winter
no eyes please

start with say her voice
or her name
or the way you met
and how everything changed from then on in

the gods gave way
and so on

another love poem
no
dahlia
a girl this time made sure of that
and some one else was watching
testing you I was she said

you failed
but won something

late nights
sex
free and fun filled
laughter-echoing sex

barefoot she came to the airport

sexy beast but tell her
when you cheat on her
she wants to know
and you do

no flower for that
no named flower
no name but the sigh of a disappointed traveler

this is where cupid comes asunder
fist in mouth arrow in foot
and all our wounds just deepened
love which once was scripted by your hand
is emailed now and dumped into the trash
deleted with no greek gods to conjure
no greek gods to conspire with
no classical allusions
no evocations or imaginings

Apollo can go and shite
and Mr. Graves keep bowing to the moon
love left you with regret

the shape of which might make an image

not floral
but empty open dark
and vegetative
with a hint of colour
from winter's end
bright then and expectant too

after all

Snow

Snow. All night. And
all day. Farms and in
the distance the sound
of an explosion to set
the avalanche off and
make it less a threat.

Morning's vast plain
cooling the face and
clearing the head.
The music from huts
rising like smoke.

Against the sky
clouds glide
like the silenced
desires of … snow.
On a branch a crow

calls out: what it says
is untranslatable.
Something to do with
the *sehnsucht* of a spring
day, something to do with love,

something to do with loss.

Nocturne

put your hand in this old hand
your lips to these drunken lips

wars are not your concern
fear not violence

I'll give you anything
let's drink

the sky opens for you
I can be your guide

take the darkness from me
you do

heal me
play the music you play

whisper to me again
of love

First Night

january is your month now
time of new beginnings
morning babe   little flower

all day you gurgled
chirped and sang happiness
into our lives

as if we had not known
such a thing
as if we had been asleep

all our lives
as if
we had been but waiting

for this and how
you broke winter's yawn
with a yawlp

and gave a hundred names
to the shiver in the air
and the colours in the sky

as if
everything was done and undone
this very morning

this very day
sung to and raised up
before so quickly the night arrived

and the hospital doors
closed to me
and so I thought

of how your heart-beat
slowed
before you were born

how frightened I was
before you were delivered
tugged-tired from your mother

how in counterpoint
my heart hurried
through the long-lived day

through the night
your first night
as I drove across the city

exiled from your swaddling
the steering-wheel brittle crumbling
and disappearing in my hands

commuted as I was
in some magical way
through the carnival

the medieval menagerie
to our first home
hungry thirsty elated and exhausted

where no one waited
cheered or cried
where the radio bleated

and the cats purred
where the newspapers grew stale
beneath my eyes

which fell closed
into sleep
o precious but wanton sleep

where I dreamt too to the image
of your new being
where my heart began to sing

and to remake itself again anew

.

www.ingramcontent.com/pod-product-compliance
Lightning Source LLC
LaVergne TN
LVHW091205080426
835509LV00006B/840